Classic Narrative Poems

Selected by Wendy Body

Contents

Longman

Edinburgh Gate
Harlow, Essex

The Man in the Moon Stayed Up Too Late

There is an inn, a merry old inn
    beneath an old grey hill,
And there they brew a beer so brown
That the Man in the Moon himself came down
    one night to drink his fill.

The ostler has a tipsy cat
    that plays a five-stringed fiddle;
And up and down he runs his bow,
Now squeaking high, now purring low,
    now sawing in the middle.

The landlord keeps a little dog
    that is mighty fond of jokes;
When there's good cheer among the guests,
He cocks an ear at all the jests
    and laughs until he chokes.

They also keep a horned cow
    as proud as any queen;
But music turns her head like ale,
And makes her wave her tufted tail
    and dance upon the green.

And O! the row of silver dishes
    and the store of silver spoons!
For Sunday there's a special pair,
And these they polish up with care
    on Saturday afternoons.

The Man in the Moon was drinking deep,
      and the cat began to wail;
A dish and a spoon on the table danced,
The cow in the garden madly pranced,
      and the little dog chased his tail.

The Man in the Moon took another mug
      and then rolled beneath his chair.
And there he dozed and dreamed of ale,
Till in the sky the stars were pale,
      and dawn was in the air.

The ostler said to his tipsy cat:
      "The white horses of the Moon,
They neigh and champ their silver bits;
But their master's been and drowned his wits,
      and the Sun'll be rising soon!"

So the cat on his fiddle played hey-diddle-diddle,
      a jig that would wake the dead;
He squeaked and sawed and quickened the tune,
While the landlord shook the Man in the Moon;
      "It's after three!" he said.

They rolled the Man slowly up the hill
      and bundled him into the Moon,
While his horses galloped up in rear,
And the cow came capering like a deer,
      and a dish ran up with a spoon.

Now quicker the fiddle went deedle-dum-diddle;
   the dog began to roar,
The cow and the horses stood on their heads;
The guests all bounded from their beds
   and danced upon the floor.

With a ping and a pong the fiddle-strings broke!
   the cow jumped over the Moon,
And the little dog laughed to see such fun,
And the Saturday dish went off at a run
   With the silver Sunday spoon.

The round Moon rolled behind the hill,
   as the Sun raised up her head.
She hardly believed her fiery eyes;
For though it was day, to her surprise
   they all went back to bed!

J. R. R. Tolkien

Tom's Angel

No-one was in the fields
But me and Polly Flint,
When, like a giant across the grass,
The flaming angel went.

It was budding time in May,
And green as green could be,
And all in his height he went along
Past Polly Flint and me.

We'd been playing in the woods,
And Polly up, and ran,
And hid her face, and said,
"Tom! Tom! The Man! The Man!"

And I up-turned; and there,
Like flames across the sky,
With wings all bristling, came
The Angel striding by.

And a chaffinch overhead
Kept whistling in the tree
while the Angel, blue as fire, came on
Past Polly Flint and me.

And I saw his hair, and all
The ruffling of his hem,
As over the clovers his bare feet
Trod without stirring them.

Polly – she cried; and, oh!
We ran, until the lane
Turned by the miller's roaring wheel,
And we were safe again.

Walter de la Mare

The Lion and Albert

There's a famous seaside place called Blackpool,
    That's noted for fresh air and fun,
And Mr and Mrs Ramsbottom,
    Went there with young Albert, their son.

A grand little lad was young Albert,
    All dressed in his best; quite a swell
With a stick with an 'orse's 'ead 'andle,
    The finest that Woolworth's could sell.

They didn't think much to the Ocean:
    The waves, they was fiddlin' and small,
There was no wrecks and nobody drownded,
    Fact, nothing to laugh at all.

So, seeking for further amusement,
    They paid and went into the Zoo,
Where they'd Lions and Tigers and Camels,
    And old ale and sandwiches too.

There were one great Lion called Wallace:
    His nose were all covered with scars –
He lay in a somnolent posture
    With the side of his face on the bars.

Now Albert had heard about Lions,
    How they was ferocious and wild –
To see Wallace lying so peaceful,
    Well, it didn't seem right to the child.

So straightway the brave little feller,
     Not showing a morsel of fear,
Took his stick with its 'orse's 'ead 'andle
     And poked it in Wallace's ear.

You could see that the Lion didn't like it,
     For giving a kind of a roll,
He pulled Albert inside the cage with 'im,
     And swallowed the little lad 'ole.

Then Pa, who had seen the occurrence,
     And didn't know what to do next,
Said "Mother! Yon Lion's 'et Albert,"
     And Mother said "Well, I am vexed!"

Then Mr and Mrs Ramsbottom –
Quite rightly, when all's said and done –
Complained to the Animal Keeper
That the Lion had eaten their son.

The keeper was quite nice about it;
He said "What a nasty mishap.
Are you sure that its *your* boy he's eaten?"
Pa said "Am I sure? There's his cap!"

The manager had to be sent for.
He came and he said "What's to do?"
Pa said "Yon Lion's 'et Albert,
And 'im in his Sunday clothes, too."

Then Mother said "Right's right, young feller;
I think it's a shame and a sin
For a lion to go and eat Albert,
And after we've paid to come in."

The manager wanted no trouble,
He took out his purse right away,
Saying "How much to settle the matter?"
And Pa said "What do you usually pay?"

But Mother had turned a bit awkward
    When she thought where her Albert had gone.
She said "No! someone's got to be summonsed" –
    So that was decided upon.

Then off they went to the P'lice Station,
    In front of the Magistrate chap;
They told 'im what happened to Albert,
    And proved it by showing his cap.

The Magistrate gave his opinion
    That no-one was really to blame
And he said that he hoped the Ramsbottoms
    Would have further sons to their name.

At that Mother got proper blazing,
    "And thank you, sir, kindly," said she.
"What, waste all our lives raising children
    To feed ruddy Lions? Not me!"

Marriott Edgar

Mrs Malone

Mrs Malone
Lived hard by a wood
All on her lonesome
As nobody should.
With her crust on a plate
And her pot on the coal
And none but herself
To converse with, poor soul.
In a shawl and a hood
She got sticks out-o'-door,
On a bit of old sacking
She slept on the floor,
And nobody, nobody
Asked how she fared
Or knew how she managed,
For nobody cared.
>   Why make a pother
>   About an old crone?
>   What for should they bother
>   With Mrs Malone?

One Monday in winter
With snow on the ground
So thick that a footstep
Fell without sound,
She heard a faint frostbitten
Peck on the pane
And went to the window
To listen again.
There sat a cock-sparrow
Bedraggled and weak,
With half-open eyelid
And ice on his beak.
She threw up the sash
And she took the bird in,
And mumbled and fumbled it
Under her chin.
>   "Ye're all of a smother,
>   Ye're fair overblown!
>   I've room fer another,"
>   Said Mrs Malone.

Come Tuesday while eating
Her dry morning slice
With the sparrow a-picking
("Ain't company nice!")
She heard on her doorpost
A curious scratch,
And there was a cat
With its claw on the latch.
It was hungry and thirsty
And thin as a lath,
It mewed and it mowed
On the slithery path.

She threw the door open
And warmed up some pap,
And huddled and cuddled it
In her old lap.
   "There, there, little brother,
   Ye poor skin-an'-bone,
   There's room fer another,"
   Said Mrs Malone.

Come Wednesday while all of them
Crouched on the mat
With a crumb for the sparrow,
A sip for the cat,
There was wailing and whining
Outside in the wood,
And there sat a vixen
With six of her brood.
She was haggard and ragged
And worn to a shred,
And her half-dozen babies
Were only half-fed,
But Mrs Malone, crying
"My! ain't they sweet!"
Happed them and lapped them
And gave them to eat.
   "You warm yerself, mother,
   Ye're cold as a stone!
   There's room fer another,"
   Said Mrs Malone.

Come Thursday a donkey
Stepped in off the road
With sores on his withers
From bearing a load.
Come Friday when icicles
Pierced the white air
Down from the mountainside
Lumbered a bear.
For each she had something,
If little, to give –
"Lord knows, the poor critters
Must all of 'em live."
She gave them her sacking,
Her hood and her shawl,
Her loaf and her teapot –
She gave them her all.
    "What with one thing and t'other
    Me fambily's grown,
    And there's room fer another,"
    Said Mrs Malone.

Come Saturday evening
When time was to sup
Mrs Malone
Had forgot to sit up.
The cat said *meeow*,
And the sparrow said *peep*,
The vixen, *she's sleeping*,
The bear, *let her sleep*.
On the back of the donkey
They bore her away.
Through trees and up mountains
Beyond night and day,
Till come Sunday morning
They brought her in state
Through the last cloudbank
As far as the Gate.
    "Who is it," asked Peter,
    "You have with you there?"
    And donkey and sparrow,
    Cat, vixen and bear

Exclaimed, "Do you tell us
Up here she's unknown?
It's our mother, God bless us!
It's Mrs Malone
Whose havings were few
And whose holding was small
And whose heart was so big
It had room for us all."
Then Mrs Malone
Of a sudden awoke,
She rubbed her two eyeballs
And anxiously spoke:
"Where am I, to goodness,
And what do I see?
My dears, let's turn back,
This ain't no place fer me!"
     But Peter said, "Mother
     go in to the Throne.
     There's room for another
     One, Mrs Malone."

Eleanor Farjeon

The Cremation of Sam McGee

There are strange things done in the midnight sun
    By the men who moil for gold;
The Arctic trails have their secret tales
    That would make your blood run cold;
The Northern Lights have seen queer sights,
    But the queerest they ever did see
Was that night on the marge of Lake Lebarge
    I cremated Sam McGee.

Now Sam McGee was from Tennessee, where the
    cotton blooms and blows.
Why he left his home in the south to roam 'round the
    Pole, God only knows.
He was always cold, but the land of gold seemed to
    hold him like a spell;
Though he'd often say in his homely way that
    "he'd sooner live in hell".

On a Christmas Day we were mushing our way over
    the Dawson trail.
Talk of your cold! through the parka's fold it stabbed
    like a driven nail.
If our eyes we'd close, then the lashes froze till
    sometimes we couldn't see;
It wasn't much fun, but the only one to whimper
    was Sam McGee.

And that very night, as we lay packed tight in our
    robes beneath the snow.
And the dogs were fed, the stars o'erhead were dancing
    heel and toe,

He turned to me, and "Cap," says he, "I'll cash in this
  trip, I guess;
And if I do, I'm asking that you won't refuse my last
  request."

Well, he seemed so low that I couldn't say no; then he
  says with a sort of moan:
"It's the cursed cold, and it's got right hold till I'm
  chilled clean through to the bone.
Yet 'tain't being dead – it's my awful dread of the icy
  grave that pains;
So I want you to swear that, foul or fair, you'll cremate
  my last remains."

A pal's last need is a thing to heed, so I swore I would
  not fail;
And we started on at the streak of dawn; but God! he
  looked ghastly pale.
He crouched on the sleigh, and he raved all day of his
  home in Tennessee;
And before nightfall a corpse was all that was left of
  Sam McGee.

There wasn't a breath in that land of death, and I
  hurried horror-driven,
With a corpse half hid that I couldn't get rid, because
  of a promise given;
It was lashed to the sleigh, and it seemed to say: "You
  may tax your brawn and brains,
But you promised true, and it's up to you to cremate
  those last remains."

Now a promise made is a debt unpaid, and the trail
  has its own stern code.

In the days to come, though my lips were dumb,
    in my heart how I cursed that load.

In the long, long night, by the lone firelight,
    while the huskies, round in a ring,

Howled out their woes to the homeless snows
    – O God! How I loathed the thing.

And every day that quiet clay seemed to
    heavy and heavier grow;

And on I went, though the dogs were spent
    and the grub was getting low;

The trail was bad, and I felt half mad,
    but I swore I would not give in;

And I'd often sing to the hateful thing,
    and it hearkened with a grin.

Till I came to the marge of Lake Lebarge,
    and a derelict there lay;

It was jammed in the ice, but I saw in a trice
    it was called the "Alice May".

And I looked at it, and I thought a bit,
    and looked at my frozen chum;

Then "Here," said I, with a sudden cry,
    "is my cre-ma-tor-eum."

Some planks I tore from the cabin floor,
    and I lit the boiler fire;

Some coal I found that was lying around,
    and I heaped the fuel higher;

The flames just soared, and the furnace
    roared – such a blaze you seldom see;

And I burrowed a hole in the glowing coal,
    and I stuffed in Sam McGee.

Then I made a hike, for I didn't like
    to hear him sizzle so;
And the heavens scowled, and the huskies
    howled, and the wind began to blow.
It was icy cold, but the hot sweat rolled down
    my cheeks, and I don't know why;
And the greasy smoke in an inky cloak went
    streaking down the sky.

I do not know how long in the snow I wrestled
    with grisly fear;
But the stars came out and they danced about
    'ere again I ventured near;
I was sick with dread, but I bravely said:
    "I'll just take a peep inside.
I guess he's cooked, and it's time I looked,"
    ... then the door I opened wide.
And there sat Sam, looking cool and calm,
    in the heart of the furnace roar;
And he wore a smile you could see a mile,
    and he said: "Please close that door.
It's fine in here, but I greatly fear you'll let
    in the cold and storm –
Since I left Plumtree, down in Tennessee,
    it's the first time I've been warm."

There are strange things done in the midnight sun
    By the men who moil for gold;
The Arctic trails have their secret tales
    That would make your blood run cold;
The Northern Lights have seen queer sights,
    But the queerest they ever did see
Was that night on the marge of Lake Lebarge
    I cremated Sam McGee.

Robert Service

Miller's End

When we moved to Miller's End,
    Every afternoon at four
A thin shadow of a shade
    Quavered through the garden-door.

Dressed in black from top to toe
    And a veil about her head
To us all it seemed as though
    She came walking from the dead.

With a basket on her arm
    Through the hedge-gap she would pass,
Never a mark that we could spy
    On the flagstones or the grass.

When we told the garden-boy
    How we saw the phantom glide,
With a grin his face was bright
    As the pool he stood beside.

"That's no ghost-walk," Billy said,
    "Nor a ghost you fear to stop –
Only old Miss Wickerby
    On a short cut to the shop."

So next day we lay in wait,
  Passed a civil time of day,
Said how pleased we were she came
  Daily down our garden-way.

Suddenly her cheek it paled,
  Turned, as quick, from ice to flame.
"Tell me," said Miss Wickerby,
  "Who spoke of me, and my name?"

"Bill the garden-boy."
    She sighed,
  Said, "Of course, you could not know
How he drowned – that very pool –
  A frozen winter – long ago."

Charles Causley

The Pelican Chorus

King and Queen of the Pelicans we;
No other Birds so grand we see!
None but we have feet like fins!
With lovely leathery throats and chins!
    Ploffskin, Pluffskin, Pelican jee,
    We think no Birds so happy as we!
    Plumpskin, Ploshkin, Pelican jill,
    We think so then, and we thought so still!

We live on the Nile. The Nile we love.
By night we sleep on the cliffs above;
By day we fish, and at eve we stand
On long bare islands of yellow sand.
And when the sun sinks slowly down
And the great rock walls grow dark and brown,
Where the purple river rolls fast and dim
And the Ivory Ibis starlike skim,
Wing to wing we dance around, –
Stamping our feet with a flumpy sound, –
Opening our mouths as Pelicans ought,
And this is the song we nightly snort: –
    Ploffskin, Pluffskin, Pelican jee,
    We think no Birds so happy as we!
    Plumpskin, Ploshkin, Pelican jill,
    We think so then, and we thought so still!

Last year came out our Daughter, Dell;
And all the Birds received her well.
To do her honour, a feast we made
For every bird that can swim or wade.
Herons and Gulls, and Cormorants black,
Cranes, and Flamingoes with scarlet back,
Plovers and Storks, and Geese in clouds,
Swans and Dilberry Ducks in crowds.
Thousands of Birds in wondrous flight!
They ate and drank and danced all night,
And echoing back from the rocks you heard
Multitude-echoes from Bird and Bird, –
    Ploffskin, Pluffskin, Pelican jee,
    We think no Birds so happy as we!
    Plumpskin, Ploshkin, Pelican jill,
    We think so then, and we thought so still!

Yes, they came; and among the rest,
The King of the Cranes all grandly dressed.
Such a lovely tail! Its feathers float
Between the ends of his blue dress-coat;
With pea-green trousers all so neat,
And a delicate frill to hide his feet, –
(For though no-one speaks of it, every one knows,
He has got no webs between his toes!)
As soon as he saw our Daughter, Dell,
In violent love that Crane King fell, –
On seeing her waddling form so fair,
With a wreath of shrimps in her short white hair.
And before the end of the next long day,
Our Dell had given her heart away;
For the King of the Cranes had won that heart,

With a Crocodile's egg and a large fish-tart.
She vowed to marry the King of the Cranes,
Leaving the Nile for stranger plains;
And away they flew in a gathering crowd
Of endless birds in a lengthening cloud.

> Ploffskin, Pluffskin, Pelican jee,
> We think no Birds so happy as we!
> Plumpskin, Ploshkin, Pelican jill,
> We think so then, and we thought so still!

And far away in the twilight sky,
We heard them singing a lessening cry, –
Farther and farther till out of sight,
And we stood alone in the silent night!
Often since, in the nights of June,
We sit on the sand and watch the moon; –
She has gone to the great Gromboolian plain,
And we probably never shall meet again!
Oft, in the long still nights of June,
We sit on the rocks and watch the moon; –
She dwells by the streams of the Chankly Bore,
And we probably never shall see her more.

> Ploffskin, Pluffskin, Pelican jee,
> We think no Birds so happy as we!
> Plumpskin, Ploshkin, Pelican jill,
> We think so then, and we thought so still!

Edward Lear

To Find a Son and Heir

A Story from Zimbabwe

A wrinkled father, more like a tortoise than
    (what in fact he was) a rich old man,
sent word that his twin sons should come to the bed
    on which he'd shortly die, and said:
"My sons, since you are twins, I've set a test
    to settle which of you had best
inherit my great fortune. Here's ten pounds
    each. Now then, I've built in the grounds
two empty rooms, identical in size,
    and whichever of you is wise
enough to fill his room chock-full, yet still
    have change out of the ten pounds, will
be heir to all I have." Now apprehensive
    of each other, the twins grew pensive
and sloped off to the dark forest's glades where
    they pondered how they should prepare
themselves for the next day's trial. Their neighbours,
    taking a holiday from their labours,
crowded about the two rooms, squinnying through
    each slit, crack, hole in order to
see which of the twins would come up with the answer.
    The first (hard-headed and no romancer)
drives up with a huge lorryful of sacks,
    crates, cartons, boxes, which he stacks
in every nook and cranny, only to discover
    that there are yawning gaps all over
and not the ghost of a hope of plugging any
    of them with his remaining penny.

All eyes now turn towards the second son,
    a dreamy youth, who hasn't done
a blind bit (so it seems) to get things ready,
    but keeps his cool amid the heady
jeers of the crowd. Entering the empty room,
    he gropes through the thronging shadows' gloom
to its still heart. There, placing it upright,
    he sets a penny candle alight,
whose beams spread out in a golden dawn
    to fill, flood and scour like a sun reborn
the room's small universe ... the crowd, grown quiet,
    begin to understand and riot,
clapping and cheering as, shoulder-high, they bear
    to the sick father his true son and heir.

Raymond Wilson

The Mistletoe Bough

The mistletoe hung in the castle hall,
The holly branch shone on the old oak wall;
And the baron's retainers were blithe and gay,
And keeping their Christmas holiday.
The baron beheld with a father's pride
His beautiful child, young Lovell's bride;
While she with her bright eyes seemed to be
The star of the goodly company.

"I'm weary of dancing now," she cried;
"Here tarry a moment – I'll hide – I'll hide!
And, Lovell, be sure thou'rt first to trace
The clue to my secret lurking place."
Away she ran – and her friends began
Each tower to search, and each nook to scan;
And young Lovell cried, "Oh where doest thou hide?
I'm lonesome without thee, my own dear bride."
They sought her that night! and they sought her next day!
And they sought her in vain when a week passed away!
In the highest – the lowest – the loneliest spot,
Young Lovell sought wildly – but found her not.
And years flew by, and their grief at last
Was told as a sorrowful tale long past,
And when Lovell appeared, the children cried,
"See! the old man weeps for his fairy bride."

At length an oak chest, that had long lain hid,
Was found in the castle – they raised the lid –
And a skeleton form lay mouldering there,
In the bridal wreath of that lady fair!
Oh! sad was her fate! – in sportive jest
She hid from her lord in the old oak chest.
It closed with a spring! and, dreadful doom,
The bride lay clasped in her living tomb!

Thomas Haynes Bayly

Lord Ullin's Daughter

A chieftain, to the Highlands bound,
    Cries, "Boatman, do not tarry,
And I'll give thee a silver pound
    To row us o'er the ferry."

"Now who be ye would cross Lochgyle,
    This dark and stormy water?"
"O, I'm the chief of Ulva's isle,
    And this Lord Ullin's daughter.

"And fast before her father's men
    Three days we've fled together,
For should he find us in the glen,
    My blood would stain the heather.

"His horsemen hard behind us ride;
    Should they our steps discover,
Then who will cheer my bonny bride
    When they have slain her lover?"

Out spoke the hardy Highland wight,
    "I'll go, my chief, I'm ready!
It is not for your silver bright;
    But for your winsome lady.

"And by my word! the bonny bird
    In danger shall not tarry;
So though the waves are raging white,
    I'll row you o'er the ferry."

By this the storm grew loud apace,
    The water-wraith was shrieking,
And in the scowl of Heaven each face
    Grew dark as they were speaking.

But still as wilder blew the wind,
    And as the night grew drearer,
Adown the glen rode armed men,
    Their trampling sounded nearer.

"O haste thee, haste!" the lady cries,
  "Though tempests round us gather;
I'll meet the raging of the skies,
  But not an angry father."

The boat has left a stormy land,
  A stormy sea before her –
When, oh! too strong, for human hand,
  The tempest gathered o'er her.

And still they rowed amidst the roar
  Of waters fast prevailing;
Lord Ullin reached that fatal shore,
  His wrath was changed to wailing.

For sore dismayed, through storm and shade,
  His child he did discover:
One lovely hand she stretched for aid,
  And one was round her lover.

"Come back! come back!" he cried in grief,
  "Across this stormy water;
And I'll forgive your Highland chief,
  My daughter! Oh, my daughter!"

'Twas vain: the loud waves lashed the shore,
  Return or aid preventing;
The waters wild went o'er his child,
  And he was left lamenting.

Thomas Campbell